BOSS LADIES OF SCIENCE

— OF —

PHILLIP MARSDEN

LOTHIAN
Children's Books

Have you ever wondered why the sky is blue, or what a black hole looks like? Are you curious about how life began, how we can live longer, or if there is life on other planets? The scientists in this book investigate all of these questions and so many more. That's what's great about science – it can answer big questions. It can tell us how things work, allow us to see new things, help us stay healthy, or even travel to the moon!

Scientists don't come any more clever, courageous and curious than the boss ladies in this book. From astronomers to zoologists, these are some of the most amazing women working in science today.

I had so much fun researching this book, finding out fascinating facts about Boss Ladies of Science, and I hope you enjoy reading about them just as much. Who knows, one of the boss scientists of the future could be you!

FROM THE AUTHOR

ANN MAKOSINSKI

You don't have to be a genius to make a difference.

A self-confessed tinkerer, Canadian Ann Makosinski has a curious mind for science, art and everything in between. When she was 15, she won the Google Science Fair for her invention of a flashlight powered by just the warmth of one's hand! She has also invented a cup that uses the energy from a hot drink to charge your phone! What will she think of next?

CATHERINE GREEN & SARAH GILBERT

British vaccinologists Dr Catherine Green and Prof Sarah Gilbert, of Oxford University, developed the AstraZeneca vaccine against the COVID-19 coronavirus. Thank you, Boss Ladies! Not only did they do this in record time during a pandemic, but they somehow managed to write a book about it, too! Sarah received a standing ovation at the Wimbledon tennis tournament in 2021 and has even had a Barbie doll made of her!

CATHY FOLEY

Aspire big, think big and bold and ask questions about how to get there, rather than thinking you have to figure it all out for yourself.

As Australia's Chief Scientist, Dr Cathy Foley advises the government on all things science, technology and innovation. This makes her the Boss Lady of Science for the whole country! And before this, she'd been the Chief Scientist at CSIRO (the Commonwealth Scientific and Industrial Research Organisation). Her work in physics has brought about barcode scanners, LED lighting, and a device that detects underground minerals worth billions of dollars!

CHANDA PRESCOD-WEINSTEIN

I'm one part of the universe that is trying to figure out another part of the universe.

Dr Chanda Prescod-Weinstein is an American theoretical physicist who could tell you a thing or two hundred about axions, neutron stars and dark matter (the invisible 'stuff' that makes up most of the universe). She is also a boss feminist theorist who campaigns against racism and sexism, and for queer, black and female inclusion in the world of physics. Shazam!

ELIZABETH BLACKBURN & CAROL GREIDER

The ability to solve complex problems is greatly enriched by having different viewpoints.

You have to repeat that good experiment just like you have to try again at the failed experiment.

Prof Elizabeth Blackburn (Australia/USA) and Dr Carol Greider (USA) won a Nobel Prize (along with Jack Szostak) for their discovery of DNA called telomeres and the enzyme telomerase. Telomeres provide protection, a bit like the caps on the ends of shoelaces, when cells divide. These bits of DNA get shorter as we get older, or through illness and stress. Telomerase helps them grow, and could be the key to a long and healthy life!

EMMA JOHNSTON

Women are socially and culturally engendered to think of maths and physics as difficult — that we don't have a natural facility with them. It's not true.

With a love of underwater worlds, especially the Great Barrier Reef and Sydney Harbour, Prof Emma Johnston is an Australian marine ecologist. She has won heaps of awards and held many Boss Lady positions at Australian universities. As if that wasn't enough, she also co-presents a TV show, *Coast Australia!*

FABIOLA GIANOTTI

Diversity is an asset of humanity, it's our richness, and we have to use it in the best possible way.

Italian Dr Fabiola Gianotti is the Boss Lady in charge at a particle physics laboratory in Switzerland called CERN. This lab has a humungous, doughnut-shaped underground tunnel, called the Large Hadron Collider. It smashes protons together at very high speeds to replicate (for our understanding) what happened at the time of the big bang – the very beginning of the universe!

FEI-FEI LI

Whatever future world we envision or we want to live in is due to the work we do today.

Dr Fei-Fei Li is a Chinese-American computer scientist specialising in artificial intelligence, also known as AI. This is when we teach computers how to think and to do things like recognise pictures! Fei-Fei works hard to make sure these computers are used ethically and reflect the thinking of diverse people in our world.

FIONA WOOD

I want people to realise that they can make a difference ... That thinking outside the box is okay – in fact, more than okay.

Prof Fiona Wood is a world-famous plastic surgeon. Plastic surgery changes the way a person's body looks or works – it can be cosmetic or reconstructive. In 2002 a lot of Australians were badly hurt in bomb attacks in Bali, Indonesia. Fiona and her team used her invention, 'spray-on skin', to treat their burns and to save lives. This led to widespread adoption of the technology and Fiona was awarded an Order of Australia.

FRANCISCA NNEKA OKEKE

As a little girl, I was fascinated by the sky; why the sky appears white at times, and blue at other times. Again, I wondered why the aeroplanes could fly... I found my vocation when I learned that physics could answer my questions.

Prof Francisca Nneka Okeke is a Nigerian physicist who specialises in the earth's upper atmosphere - the ionosphere - and its potential effects on climate change. She is Professor of Physics at the University of Nigeria and was the first ever female head of a department there. She aims to encourage more girls to study science in Africa, knowing it will benefit society as a whole.

GINA MOSELY

Dr Gina Mosely is a climate researcher from England. She goes on expeditions to faraway places, like northern Greenland, where she abseils into caves to find very old minerals called calcites. The calcites have layers, like tree rings, that Gina examines to learn about the climate of the distant past and what we might expect in the future!

HINDOU OUMAROU IBRAHIM

Women are experts on many issues, not only on women's issues.

Hindou Oumarou Ibrahim is an environmentalist and climate activist from Chad in Central Africa. She works with her pastoralist community to make 2D and 3D maps to help locate resources like fresh water for their cattle. She's a champion of Indigenous knowledge and women's voices in the fight against climate change.

JANE GOODALL

You matter and have a role to play. You make a difference of some sort every single day, and you have a choice as to whether you will make this a better world, even in a small way, by making the right choices.

Dr Jane Goodall is an English primatologist. That's someone who studies primates, such as monkeys, gorillas and orangutans. In Jane's case she is an expert on chimpanzees! She lived with them in Tanzania, Africa, and has made many new discoveries about the species. She founded the Jane Goodall Institute to protect the chimpanzees and their environment, and its offshoot, Roots and Shoots, to educate and empower young people to improve our world.

JENNIFER DOUDNA & EMMANUELLE CHARPENTIER

Embrace your interests, your passions, and really give it your all!

When you're a researcher...in a way you're a detective because you have some questions and puzzles to go through.

Dr Jennifer Doudna (USA) and Prof Emmanuelle Charpentier (France) won the 2020 Nobel Prize in Chemistry for their discoveries in CRISPR-Cas9 (a what now?) – a way to precisely edit DNA. Scientists can use this tool to modify genes to help cure disease, make seedless fruit, mosquitoes that don't bite, or maybe even to bring back the woolly mammoth!

KATIE BOUMAN

If you're excited and willing to put in the extra work, you can make things happen that others don't expect.

American astronomer Prof Katie Bouman was part of the team that captured the first ever image of a black hole! She helped write a computer program that turned data from radio telescopes into a picture we can all see. (You can't get close enough to a black hole to take a photo with your phone. If you did, it would suck you in and turn you into spaghetti. Yikes!)

KIARA NIRGHIN

Having more young girls in STEM will bring growth to innovation-related industries, and benefit many communities.

Kiara Nirghin is an innovative inventor from South Africa. When she was 16, Kiara won the grand prize at the Google Science Fair for her invention of a superabsorbent polymer made from organic materials such as orange peel. The polymer can hold hundreds of times its own weight in water, so it helps when growing crops in times of drought.

KIRSTEN BANKS

I want to show everyone that you can achieve your dreams no matter what!

Indigenous Australian astrophysicist Kirsten Banks loves to talk about space! She is very proud of her Wiradjuri roots and the rich history of Aboriginal astronomy, which dates back over 65 000 years! Blending the old with the new she also makes awesome, science-y TikTok videos!

MAE JEMISON

I think it's so vitally important that all people in this world are involved in the process of discovery.

American Dr Mae Jemison was the first ever woman of colour to go into space. She did this aboard the space shuttle *Endeavour* in 1992. One of her inspirations to become an astronaut was the show *Star Trek*. Not only did she go on to star in an episode herself, but she is also helping to create the real-life USS *Enterprise* with the 100-Year Starship project. Out of this world!

MARGARET HAMILTON

Don't let fear get in the way and don't be afraid to say 'I don't know' or 'I don't understand'— no question is a dumb question.

Dr Margaret Hamilton is a computer scientist and software engineer from the USA. In 1969, Margaret and her team wrote the code that helped the Apollo mission land safely on the moon! All the code was printed on big stacks of paper because the computers then were much less powerful than your average phone today!

MAY-BRITT MOSER

I am very curious about things...
It gives me so much pleasure when I understand
something that I did not understand before.

Dr May-Britt Moser is a neuroscientist from Norway. A neuroscientist studies the
brain and the nervous system to understand how they work. May-Britt won a
Nobel Prize in 2014 for her discovery of 'grid cells'. These are our brains' way
of knowing where we are, so we don't fall over or walk into a wall!

MERRITT MOORE

All the work and intention you put into a dream will pay off (not always in the way you think — but in a way which is just as exciting and rewarding).

American Dr Merritt Moore is a quantum physicist with university degrees from Harvard and Oxford. Oh, and she is also a professional ballet dancer! Mind. Blown. She loves to mix art and science to think creatively in the lab, and to apply the laws of motion to her dance moves. She has even done choreographed dances with robots!

MICHELLE DICKINSON (NANOGIRL)

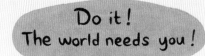

Dr Michelle Dickinson is a nanotechnologist and educator based in New Zealand. She is passionate about communicating the wonders of science and lighting the fire for STEM in as many people as possible. Her superhero alter ego Nanogirl (whose superpowers come from studying STEM) uses books, videos, live shows and even birthday parties to educate and inspire.

MICHELLE SIMMONS

Women think differently and that diversity is invaluable.

British-born Prof Michelle Simmons leads the way in atomic electronics (very small) and quantum computing (very fast!). Michelle moved to Australia in 1999 and, among loads of honours and awards, was named Australian of the Year in 2018. She is a big supporter of young girls and boys getting into science. In the future you might even use one of her super-duper quantum computers!

SARA SEAGER

Listen to your own inner voice and not what others say. Work hard. Find something you love doing that you are also good at.

Prof Sara Seager is an astronomer and planetary scientist from Canada, who is based in the USA. She is an expert on exoplanets (planets outside of our solar system) and their atmospheres. If the gases there are like the ones we have here on Earth, maybe, just maybe, there could be life on other planets!

SIOUXSIE WILES

Study what you are passionate about. But be the kind of person who uses your skills to make a difference in the world.

Dr Siouxsie Wiles is very bright, in more ways than one! She loves bioluminescence, which is when things like jellyfish, fireflies or even bacteria produce light. She studies glowing bacteria and viruses to find new medicines. And that's not the only way she helps stop disease. With Toby Morris she made cool cartoons that showed us how to slow the spread of the COVID-19 virus. They were so good she was named 2021's New Zealander of the Year!

TARA McALLISTER

When you have a different world view, you see the world differently, you ask questions differently, you come up with solutions differently.

Dr Tara McAllister (Te Aitanga ā Māhaki/ Ngāti Porou) is a freshwater ecologist, who studies things like poisonous algae in the rivers of New Zealand. She combines modern science with Mātauranga Māori – the traditional knowledge of her ancestors – and is passionate about Indigenous peoples' inclusion and participation in science and education.

TEBELLO NYOKONG

Being a scientist means being in touch with your environment, having an inquisitive mind and asking questions about how things work.

Prof Tebello Nyokong is a South African chemist who grew up tending sheep in the mountains of Lesotho. Fascinated by the natural world around her, she wanted to study science. Tebello's research focuses on an alternative cancer treatment that uses a blue dye, like you would find in jeans. When the dye is targeted by a laser it emits oxygen that can kill harmful cancer cells.

TU YOUYOU

Every scientist dreams of doing something that can help the world.

Tu Youyou is a chemist from China. In the 1970s she found a remedy for a disease called malaria. Looking to ancient herbal medicine recipes, she extracted an ingredient from a herb called sweet wormwood and tested it on herself. It worked! It is used to this day in anti-malarial drugs that have saved millions of lives! Her great work wasn't celebrated until years later when she won the Nobel Prize in 2015.

VEENA SAHAJWALLA

> If you have something exciting to bring to the table, you don't have to be afraid to speak up.

Prof Veena Sahajwalla is an inventor and materials scientist from India, who is based in Australia. She is passionate about recycling and creating value from waste. She has figured out ways to use old tyres to make steel and to use old clothes to make furniture and building materials! What a legend.

Dedicated to all the Boss Ladies of Science who came before.

A Lothian Children's Book
Published in Australia and Aotearoa New Zealand in 2022
by Hachette Australia
(an imprint of Hachette Australia Pty Limited)
Gadigal Country, Level 17, 207 Kent Street, Sydney NSW 2000
www.hachettechildrens.com.au

Hachette Australia acknowledges and pays our respects to the past, present and future Traditional Owners and Custodians of Country throughout Australia and recognises the continuation of cultural, spiritual and educational practices of Aboriginal and Torres Strait Islander peoples. Our head office is located on the lands of the Gadigal people of the Eora Nation.

Text and illustrations copyright © Phillip Marsden 2022

A catalogue record for this book is available from the National Library of Australia

ISBN: 978 0 7344 2122 7 (hardback)

Designed by Christabella Designs
Printed in China by 1010 Printing